Summer in South Georgia

Jamie Grant

Limited First Edition of only 600 copies
signed by the Author

12/600

Watermill Books

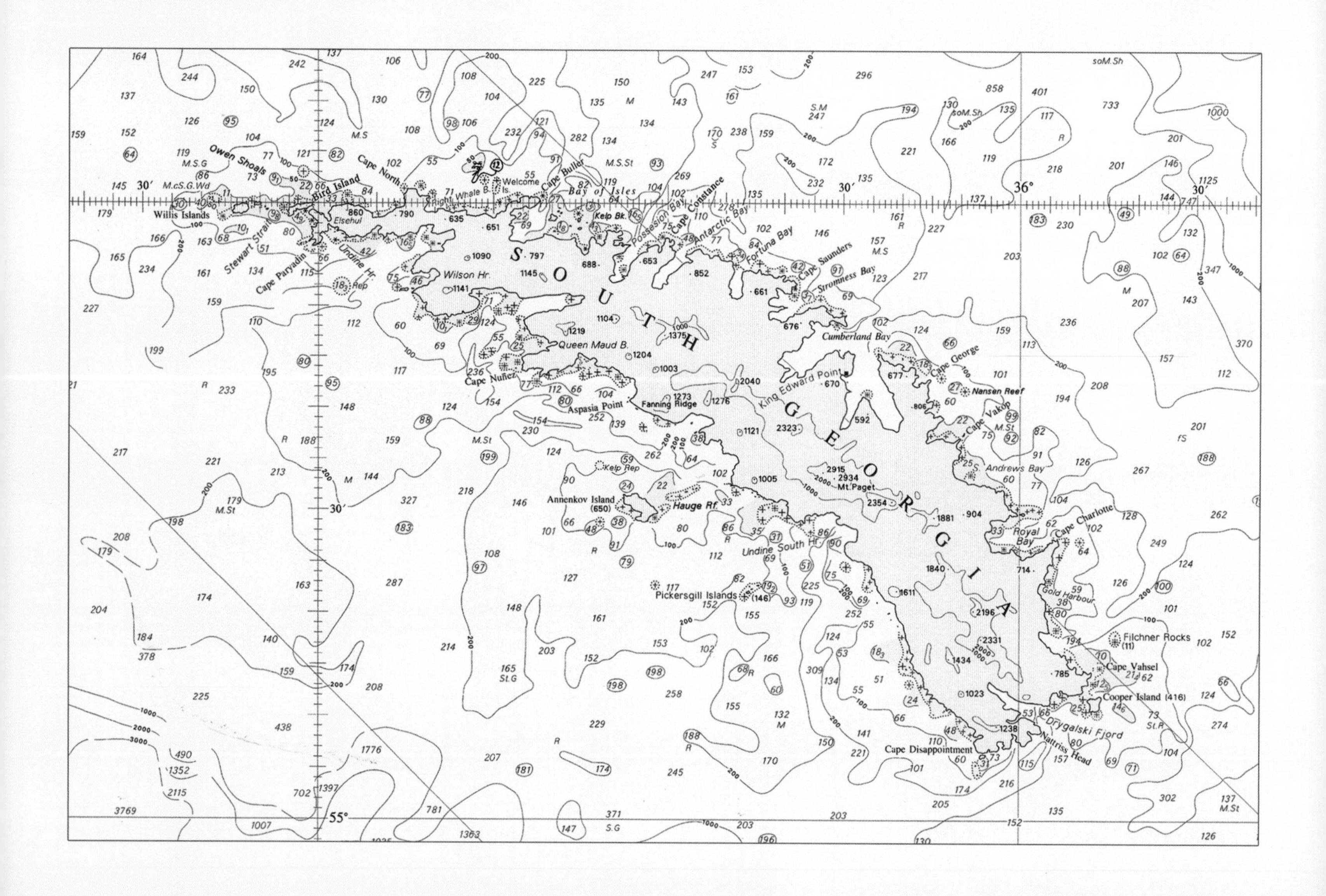
SOUTH GEORGIA
Owen Shoals
Bird Island
Willis Islands
Stewart Strait
Cape Paryadin
Undine Hr.
Elsehul
Cape North
Right Whale B.
Welcome Is.
Cape Buller
Bay of Isles
Kelp Bk.
Possession Bay
Cape Constance
Antarctic Bay
Fortuna Bay
Cape Saunders
Stromness Bay
Wilson Hr.
Queen Maud B.
Cape Nuñez
Aspasia Point
Fanning Ridge
Cumberland Bay
King Edward Point
Cape George
Nansen Reef
Cape Vakop
S. Andrews Bay
Mt. Paget
Kelp Rep
Annenkov Island (650)
Hauge Rf.
Undine South Hr.
Royal Bay
Cape Charlotte
Gold Harbour
Pickersgill Islands (146)
Filchner Rocks (11)
Cape Vahsel
Cooper Island (416)
Drygalski Fjord
Nattriss Head
Cape Disappointment
36°
55°
30′

Foreword

South Georgia is one of the world's most spectacular places. Rising sheer out of the South Atlantic Ocean, it is a hundred-mile long mountain range, a geological outlier of the Andes.

The magnificence of the scenery is matched by the wildlife. The island teems with seals, penguins and seabirds, while whales cruise offshore.

South Georgia is also the site of remarkable human endeavour. The story of Ernest Shackleton's boat journey from Elephant Island to South Georgia, and his crossing of the island, is the stuff of legend.

The whaling industry thrived on South Georgia from 1904 to the mid 1960s. However much one might deplore the impact of whaling, the story of the men (and the few women) who lived and worked – and in many cases died – in this remote and hostile environment is also one of human courage and adventure.

The former whaling stations, monuments to the heavy industry which once existed there, are deteriorating rapidly in South Georgia's extreme climate.

However, the natural environment is experiencing a remarkable recovery. The whale population is growing, and reindeer (introduced by the whalers for food and sport, and the cause of much damage to the native flora) have recently been removed.

Rats and mice, inadvertently introduced from sealing and whaling ships over two centuries, decimated the island's bird population. But in recent years they have been the target of the world's largest ever rodent eradication project, undertaken by the South Georgia Heritage Trust (SGHT), a small Scottish charity based in Dundee.

Costing some £7.5 million, the eradication has been funded entirely from donations raised by the Trust, and was completed in 2015. If it has succeeded (the signs are good) South Georgia is now free of rodents for the first time in 200 years and on its way back to the pristine state in which Captain Cook discovered it in 1775.

Birds are already returning to places where they have not been seen within living memory. Scientists estimate that numbers could eventually increase by as much as 100 million, making South Georgia one of the world's most important seabird sanctuaries.

I am delighted that Jamie was able to spend several weeks on South Georgia as SGHT's 'artist in residence'. Readers can discover more information about the Trust at www.sght.org.

Howard Pearce
Commissioner for South Georgia, 2002–2006
Chairman, South Georgia Heritage Trust, 2006–2016

Introduction

My journey to South Georgia started many years ago at my father's bookshelf. Idling through the dusty hardbacks of travel and distant adventure, Shackleton's *South* practically jumped off the shelf. The spine was so broken that it fell open in my hands like the wings of a moth.

I was gripped by Shackleton's incredible account of how his ship *Endurance* became trapped among the splintering pack-ice of the Weddell Sea, the subsequent voyage from Elephant Island to South Georgia and the desperate mountain crossing to reach the whaling station at Stromness Bay. Most of all I was struck by the compassion Shackleton showed towards his men.

Antarctica had hovered at the back of my consciousness ever since, vivid in my imagination but surely too far for an ordinary mortal like myself to ever reach. A BBC documentary on Britain's whale hunters, with its spectacular backdrop of South Georgia's ice blue seas and frozen mountains, caught my photographer's eye and reignited an old longing. I became fixated on the possibility of travelling to this remote corner of the world.

I finally reached South Georgia with the help and support of the South Georgia Heritage Trust (SGHT), which accepted me on their Artist in Residence programme in 2015. I made the long journey from Scotland to Cumberland Bay in the north of the island where I lived with the staff who ran the museum and shop in Grytviken. Surrounded by the rusting remains of an old whaling station, we had to walk around the bay to the British Antarctic Survey (BAS) base at King Edward Point for supplies.

My brief seemed simple enough - to explore as much of the island as possible with a notepad and a camera. But nothing could have prepared me for a summer of such relentless adventure. I am hugely grateful to both the Government of South Georgia and the South Sandwich Islands (GSGSSI) and to BAS staff for their help getting me through hostile waters and terrain to remote locations on neighbouring peninsulas.

I wanted to share this extraordinary experience of an austral summer on South Georgia. So I have combined extracts from my journal with photographs to give a fleeting impression of the island's landscapes, wildlife and people.

South Georgia and Antarctica remain truly wild and a testament to the tenacious resilience of nature. Despite the harshest of conditions and centuries of over-exploitation by both sealers and whalers, the wildlife on the island is now so abundant that I spent much of my time dodging it. Yet it is still an incredibly fragile habitat, and I was shocked by the sheer scale of glacial retreat, driven by climate change, around the island.

As well as the SGHT, BAS and the GSGSSI there are a few individuals that I would like to thank for making this journey and book possible. Howard Pearce for his advice from the start. Kevin and Jayne Ramage at The Watermill Bookshop for their enduring support and patience and for publishing this book on my return. David Harbott and Jo Cound for their design and photo editing.

Most important of all I would like to dedicate *Summer in South Georgia* to Fiona and Tom, for holding the fort through a Highland winter and welcoming me back from the south with open arms.

Jamie Grant

Departure

There are few places left in the world where you have no alternative other than to travel five days by sea to reach your destination. The *Pharos SG*, the fisheries protection vessel responsible for South Georgia, throws its lines and pulls out of safe harbour in the Falkland Islands.

While still in calmer waters we have to endure emergency muster training, which involves a young sailor squeezing like a contortionist into a bright red, rubber immersion suit. I quickly conclude that I would be at the bottom of the ocean long before I had managed to get it above my knees.

Despite the direst of predictions of hellish crossings and giant waves, it is flat calm with balmy evening sunshine out on deck. Three Peal's Dolphins bow ride in front of the ship. A single Magellan Penguin porpoises through the water and seabirds start making looping trails off the stern of the boat.

Leafing through a bird book on the bridge I excitedly identify my first Southern Fulmar, Antarctic Petrel, Cape (painted) Petrel and a tiny Wilson's Storm Petrel that dances in the waves to pick out food. Time slips and the ocean takes on a silvery quality,
like liquid mercury.

PSSU 31 22 7

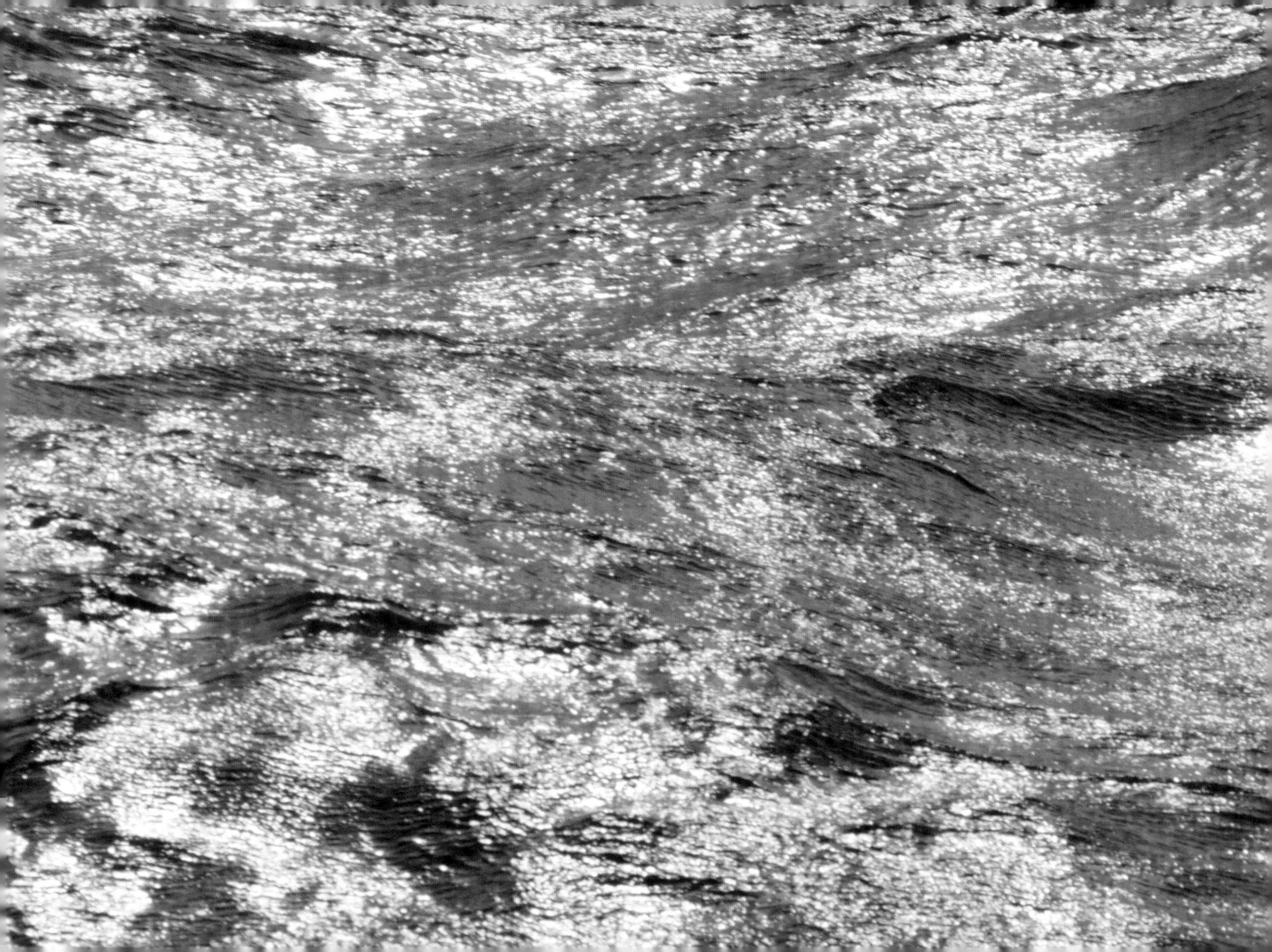

The Convergence

This evening we cross the Antarctic Convergence, where warmer currents meet cooler waters and produce a rich upwelling of nutrients and marine life. There is no clear delineation to this amorphous crossing into Antarctic waters. Only a low sea mist on the horizon and the tick down of the thermometer that the crew occasionally hang into the sea from the bridge.

But for me the idea of ‘The Convergence’ holds fantastical possibilities. Out there, beyond the thin veil of low mist, I picture the gargantuan sea monsters that populated old maritime maps and the white continent that drew so many explorers south for knowledge, glory or ruin.

The Crossing

It is bitingly cold outside so I slip back onto the serenity of the bridge. A long row of windows stretch around for maximum visibility. The Captain and his watchman stand on duty in front of banks of buttons, levers, radar screens, roll meters and other gadgets. There is a pot plant, music in the background and always a brew and cigarette to be had on the step outside, huddling from the wind.

Although the light outside is failing, both men keep their eyes glued firmly to the sea. This far south it is much more than maritime traffic that they have to be vigilant for. The radar picks up tiny, static blips up to 12 miles away that eventually hove into enormous icebergs on the distant horizon. Through powerful binoculars we can make out precipitous cliffs, cornices and sculptured peaks that will never be scaled. Some are flat topped or 'tabular' because they are hewn off the ice sheet. They are like lost continents, brooding and magnificent.

We keep a safe distance but the real fear for the crew is shards of rotten ice that calve off and lie in wait just under the surface. The crew call the bigger pieces 'growlers' and the smaller ones 'burgy bits' and they could cut through our single skinned steel hull like a tin opener.

The Captain switches a brilliant conical spotlight onto the waters in front of the boat. The crew work in rotation throughout the night, scanning the waves ahead. With clearer skies the Southern Cross appears, a beacon for long nights of distant dreaming in the Southern Ocean.

Cumberland Bay

First light falls on South Georgia. I make it onto the deck at 4am to be met by a long chain of snow-capped mountains rising mournfully out of the sea. The island is swathed in cloud but I can still make out fiords, inlets, ice fields and crooked peaks. It is my first true wilderness – a landscape that remains essentially unaltered since James Cook first set eyes on it back in 1775 and wrote:

> *"The wild rocks raised their lofty summits till they were lost in cloud and the valleys laid buried in snow. Not a tree or shrub was to be seen, not even big enough for a toothpick."*

As we round the British Antarctic Survey base at King Edward Point the wide and sheltered Cumberland Bay opens up ahead of us. At the far end are the ramshackle remains of the old whaling station of Grytviken, tucked in the shadow of the snow-scarred Mount Hodges. We are met on the slipway by slumbering baby Elephant Seals, Fur Seals, a King Penguin and a South Georgia government officer sporting an orange hard hat.

Grytviken

My ‘home’ for the next seven weeks in South Georgia is among the rusting remains of a ghost town with a fascinating and terrible past. Built by the Norwegian captain and entrepreneur CA Larsen for the sole purpose of hunting and processing whales, Grytviken could dissect and boil down as many as 25 whales for their lucrative oil in a single day.

With seven such stations built on South Georgia, a total of 175,250 whales were processed on the island in the 50 years after the first whale was towed to shore in 1904. By the time Grytviken was abandoned in 1971 the Humpback, Right, Baleen, Fin, and Blue whales of the Southern Ocean had been hunted to the point of extinction. Although slow to recover whale sightings have increased in these waters in recent years.

Grytviken is still littered with the rusting remains of the whaling industry. Walk around it and you can almost hear the clink of heavy chains as carcasses were winched onto the shore. The flensers peeling back the blubber with their long blades and lemmers working huge steam saws to divide up the whales and feed the constantly hungry boilers located beneath the meat and the bone lofts. Over it all hung the pall of rotting flesh.

Even in its heyday Sir Ernest Shackleton described Grytviken as 'a strange and curious place'. Bones still scatter the bay and three stranded abandoned whale catchers, the *Dias*, *Albatross* and *Petrel* (its harpoon still fixed), loom over the shore. An eerie stillness often creeps in with darkness. I imagine the souls of both the whales and the whalers that perished holding silent council between the aisles of rusting machinery. On a windy night I stand in the old wooden church and listen to the timber creak around me, like a ship straining to break its moorings.

Shackleton's Grave

The snow has come as a reminder that, even in summer, the winter never really leaves South Georgia. It swirls across the bay and stings my face in the small graveyard, the last resting place of drowned whalers, an Argentine submariner and Britain's most celebrated explorer, Sir Ernest Shackleton.

Famed for his epic crossing of South Georgia in 1916 to save his men stranded on Elephant Island, he returned five years later hoping to circumnavigate the entire Antarctic continent. Only this time an ailing Shackleton limped into South Georgia in a ship dogged with engine trouble and with dark financial clouds on the horizon. He died suddenly in Cumberland Bay of a heart attack onboard *Quest* on 5 January 1922, aged just 47.

When asked by the *Daily Graphic* before he sailed on this final, ill-fated journey why he chose to be an explorer, Shackleton talked about the lure of the south almost like an addiction that would inevitably catch up with him:

> *"One goes once and then one gets the fever and can't stop going. So I return to the wild again and again, until I suppose in the end the wild will win."*

The sun cuts across Gull Lake, fingers along the lower slopes of Mount Hodges and delicately picks out the rows of white crosses against deep shadow. Light flecks of snow still fall as I press the camera shutter on a landscape torn between winter and spring. Where else could Shackleton, adventurer and poet at heart, find ultimate solace than on this Antarctic isle?

Harpon Bay

I walk with British Antarctic Survey scientists Steph and Jamie over Echo Pass to Harpon on the far side of Thatcher Peninsula. It is a long traverse over the snowy saddle and down to the wide bay where the Lyell glacier meets the sea. Harpon Hut sits just back from the beach, a tiny refuge from the elements with blue plastic plates and mugs for hot soup and whisky-laced tea.

We have come to Harpon to survey the breeding success of Petrels, South Georgia's pre-historic scavengers. They are the ultimate opportunists who pick any carcass to the bone, steal penguin eggs and even pluck flesh from a slumbering Fur Seal's open wound.

And yet there is something oddly compelling about the Northern and Southern Giant Petrels that makes them popular with British Antarctic Scientists. They have piercing green eyes and huge tubular beaks. For all their menace and grace in the air they have to run like drunken sailors downhill to get enough speed up to take off.

Back in the lab Jamie and Steph painstakingly dissect an adult male that has died in a collision with a ship. Its liver will be sent back to Cambridge to be tested for toxins. At the top of the food chain, Giant Petrels are key indicators of the build up of a cocktail of man-made chemicals even in this far-flung corner of the world.

Rab

Ice at Harpon

Sitting on the beach at Harpon, I am looking at a chunk of sculptured ice that has being driven onto the pebbles by the surf. Its provenance fascinates me. Maybe this is the fractured remains of ice that has fallen off the front of the Lyell Glacier a few hundred yards away. The Lyell is in tumultuous retreat, giving off the odd rumble as another slab calves off into the sea.

But what is there to divine from this particular fragment of ice? How deep did the snow fall to form it? How long has it been held in stasis within a vast frozen river and what would those tiny air bubbles trapped inside tell us about the life and atmosphere of the distant past? Even as I am forming the questions the ice is melting, ebbing back to water. The sky is dull and overcast and yet it shines across millennia like dusking glass.

Back at the King Edward Point bar we chip glacial ice into our gin and tonics and listen for it to fizz and pop like Rice Krispies.

Discovery Bay

Discovery Bay opens out from a high vantage point on the shoulder of Brown Mountain. Below the sea is fringed with a wide swathe of boggy tussock grass with Penguin River meandering from the Hamberg Lakes down to the beach. The afternoon sun reflects off the sea as though it is beaten metal.

A pair of Sooty Albatrosses pick up the thermals and make long passes past the rocky bluffs below me. I love the arched curve of their slender wings and their fine charcoal tones. The female perches on the grassy crook of an outcrop of rock and throws her head back in a long, crooning call. Soon they will be rearing chicks and straying as far south as the ice-choked Weddell Sea in search of food.

I hear the williwaw gusting off Sugar Top Mountain long before it reaches me. The glacial blast funnels down the valley like a freight train. When it hits it bends the grasses around me flat to the ground. The cold indifference of the white mountain cuts straight through me and I feel every inch of the 9,000 miles from home.

Jet Boats

There is no transport around the island other than by boat or foot. So the British Antarctic Survey have two jet boats and a couple of Zodiacs to get scientists into remote locations on neighbouring peninsulas. They operate in narrow weather windows, so speed is everything and there is usually some chop to the water. We go on white-knuckle rides, bouncing across the waves to be dropped off with heavy bags on shores littered with floating ice.

As there is spare time we glide in to see how close we can safely edge up to the sheer face of a glacier. One of the crew then takes a GPS location to track its retreat year on year. It is a nervy moment. Boatmen Matthew and Russ keep their hand on the throttle and an eye on a quick exit, just in case a huge slab of ice calves into the sea and we have to outrun a mini tsunami wave.

HUMBER
LUNA

SUZANNA HUT

Suzanna's Hut

We cut through choppy water on the jet boat and a Zodiac with South Georgia's longest standing residents, Pat and Sarah Lurcock. They are off on a short break to Carlita Bay, one of the most secluded holiday spots on the planet. We drop them off in the sheltered cove with supplies of food, fuel and a satellite phone.

The hut is basic but well equipped with proper bunk beds, a primus stove and a tilly lantern. Their pick-up is weather dependent so there are emergency rations of freeze dried mince and Smash in an old ammunition box, together with trashy novels, just in case of delay. Pat and Sarah wave us off beaming with excitement.

Most of the huts around Cumberland Bay, maintained to provide food and shelter for field scientists, are known by their location on the map. Suzanna's Hut is the exception. It is named after the daughter of one of the trustees of the South Georgia Heritage Trust who was first brought here as a baby. Prints of her tiny hand and foot with a date are set above the window.

LUNA
HUMBER

Pelagic Australis

I've been lucky enough to hitch a ride with one of the expedition yachts that stop in at Grytviken's safe harbour. The *Pelagic Australis* has been chartered by a group of Italians who are on a hiking holiday on the island. They invited me along for a walk around the side of the Nordenskjöld Glacier.

Before now I have only looked down on the glaciers in South Georgia from mountain passes or skirted close to them in boats. Neither gives a true impression of their scale. As we walk up to the flank of the Nordenskjöld its bold sweep of elemental force cuts across my entire field of view. The mountains behind seem dwarfed.

As we approach the side of the glacier it becomes animated, alive. Pools gather and run off its sides with a deep burbling of water in the fissures and pressure cracks that criss-cross the superstructure. It is like some gargantuan, wild animal that lies wounded, slowly dying. Glaciers like Nordenskjöld are shrinking fast all over South Georgia as climate change gathers pace, some by as much as two to three kilometres a year.

We cross a moraine of crushed rock abandoned by the glacier. When the slope gets too steep I'm forced to abandon the dark earth and step onto an alien world. It is the strangest of feelings, walking on an ancient flow of ice, camouflaged by a dusting of rocks and soil. Successive, narrow crevasses open up in the last metres to the glacier's face. At the lip a huge slab of rotten ice has broken off and leans into thin air, hanging in suspended animation. Far below the bay is littered with shattered, dusty blue remains.

Storm

Only now do I really understand what it means to be in the Antarctic Polar region. Gone are the clear days when we sat outside in sunglasses and t-shirts for breakfast and worried about getting burnt by the high UV. Ragged winter has returned with a vengeance.

I'm wrapped in a sleeping bag next to the radiator in my office drinking a cup of tea and I am still cold. The snow blizzards horizontally outside my window in tremendous rolling gusts. The sea outside has receded to a thumb smudge on empty canvas. When the wind drops the snow thickens and falls in white petals. The view clears for a moment onto streets of rusting whaling machinery with Fur Seals sledging around town on their bellies.

ANNO
1913

The Repeater

Ray stands at the top of the mountain clutching a white, flexible pole that looks like it could be a lightning rod, or maybe a modern day druid's staff. It is in fact an antenna for the radio repeater on the top of a mountain ridge above King Edward's Point. It is an essential piece of kit for scientific field parties to communicate with base from more remote terrain via VHS radio.

Ray has learned to turn his hand to anything in his role of technician for the British Antarctic Survey base. His work ranges from small jobs like emptying filters in washing machines, to maintaining the hydro plant and electricity supply to the entire island. Last week he brought around makeshift disco lighting and a glitter ball (run off an old car battery) for an improvised party in one of the old whalers' sheds.

Today he is standing at the top of the hill like Moses in the swirling mist, trying for the fourth day running to fix the repeater. When all attempts to patch it up fail once again he coolly informs the base commander on the local radio channel that he has had enough. He says he is going to throw the lot off the side of the cliff into the sea. He then slowly and deliberately unscrews the receivers from the silver case that protects them from the elements and loads them into his rucksack.

Before hoisting the lot onto his back to take down and repair in his workshop, Ray pauses to look around. His mood lifts as the mist clears to reveal the shifting patina of aquamarine sea far below. 'Not a bad spot for a day's work' he says with a smile and a sweep of his hand and begins the long walk back down to base.

The Flats

Ilaria stops for a moment from her walk to inspect a small burrow in the grass at her feet. It is no more than a few inches wide and runs several feet back under the ground. After a close inspection she marks this Diving Petrel nest down as unoccupied, takes a GPS coordinate and continues to walk her narrow transect line across the wide plain between the Hamberg Lakes and the ocean.

Ilaria is a field assistant, contracted by the South Georgia Government to monitor two of South Georgia's ground-nesting birds, Diving Petrels and Antarctic Prions. With no defence from the egg thieving rats that colonised the island from passing ships, many birds have all but stopped breeding on the main island.

Hopefully this is set to change after an ambitious eradication project by the South Georgia Heritage Trust to rid the island of rats. Over several phases the affected sections of the island were baited with poison by helicopter. The South Georgia Government is now monitoring to check there aren't any rats left, as well as track the expected recovery of ground-nesting birds.

I decide to scramble up onto a high ridge on Mount Osmond to watch Ilaria's deliberate progress from above. The Norwegians fancifully called the wide glacial basin in front of the Hamberg Lakes 'Hestesletten', the horses' plain. From my vantage point I can also see why the whalers imagined horses galloping with wild manes across these yellowing grasslands, bound only by mountains and sea.

Ilaria methodically criss-crosses the flats in straight lines. Her task may be scientific but there is also something poetic about her pensive navigation of way markers across the landscape. A tiny, concentrated line in a broad sweep of light.

Maiviken

Maiviken, named May Bay by the Norwegian whalers, is a short hike over Dead Man's Pass from Cumberland Bay. From the bare mountains at Dead Man's you drop into a sheltered wildlife haven. There are coves with plenty of beaches for Elephant and Fur Seals to ferociously protect their harems of mothers with pups. Further back in the deep tussock grass are nesting Pintail Ducks, Skuas, Giant Petrels, a colony of Gentoo Penguins and the high trill of the tiny South Georgia Pipit.

Every other day biologist Jamie braves all weathers to walk over from the British Antarctic Survey (BAS) base to monitor the health of these animals. He photographs the seal colonies, collects their scat (he has a weekly quota) to analyse their diet and weighs the seal pups to chart their growth.

Jamie also keeps a watchful eye over the breeding progress of the Gentoo colony. This summer most of the Gentoo Penguins at Maiviken have abandoned their nests, leaving the ground scattered with dead chicks. It is a similar story at the other BAS base at Bird Island to the west where not a single chick has survived from a colony of 4,000 nests.

At the back of these colony collapses hangs the spectre of climate change. If the penguins or seals are struggling it is probably down to a shortage of Antarctic shrimp or krill, the bread and butter of the entire food chain. Shrinking winter sea ice around the Antarctic peninsula is reducing the krill nursery grounds and possibly affecting their northerly density and distribution in South Georgian waters.

Walking around with Jamie I realise that here in the Southern Ocean we are on the sharp end of climate change, where the smallest of margins can have devastating consequences for fragile wildlife communities.

The Macs at the Rookery

Looking down towards Rookery Point from a high mountain pass I could swear we are joining the South West coastal path in the United Kingdom. The rocky headland is swathed with green grass and the sea looks inviting despite a blanket of low cloud.

Except there are a couple of small anomalies. I can just make out the outrageous chatter of a Macaroni Penguin colony on the rocks at the end of the headland. And there is a blue iceberg floating out in the bay. After a sudden twang, like the snap of a high-tension cable, the iceberg rolls over in a languorous half somersault. I watch a circular wave ripple out around the bay and conclude that actually this could only be South Georgia.

Down at the Macaroni colony BAS biologists Steph and Jamie are busy counting breeding pairs and resetting the camera trap. I sit and watch the garrulous birds jostle for position in the colony and marvel at their huge personalities. With their greased-back flash of yellow hair and sharp dress code these guys are definitely the plucky little gangsters of the penguin world.

Wanderers

Said to represent the soul of the sailor, no other sea bird can trace such a magnificent arc of feathered will over silvering seas. I saw my first Wandering Albatross on the outward voyage from Stanley. Despite keeping a wary distance from the boat there was no mistaking the vast wingspan and measured economy of this magnificent creature's beat-less flight. Once fledged, the juveniles live their first two or three years on the wing and can circumnavigate the entire Southern Ocean in less than six months.

Wandering Albatrosses nest on the smaller islands around South Georgia and their populations are monitored on Prion, Albatross, and Bird islands. On Bird Island their numbers have fallen by 30 per cent in the past 30 years and they are now considered to be critically endangered worldwide. This is largely due to thousands of birds getting caught up and drowned in the long lines of the toothfish, tuna and swordfish fisheries every year.

I made it to Prion on a Zodiac from the *Pharos* patrol ship with BAS scientist Lewis. To get there we had to clamber down a rope ladder in cumbersome survival suits into the rib. Our driver expertly negotiated rafts of kelp to land us on a narrow black sand beach, teeming with angry Fur Seals.

We jumped into the shallow water and fought our way to the top of the beach, fending off lunging males from every angle with walking poles. We had just reached safer ground when the Captain called us back to the ship to avoid getting lost in rolling sea fog. This made for the briefest of wildlife encounters. I had just enough time to run up the long boardwalk with Lewis, still in our heavy orange immersion suits, to an observation platform at the top of the island.

From here I took a couple of photographs of a juvenile Albatross on a nest, waiting for a parent to return with food. The Wanderer observed me coolly with a beady eye, seemingly unconcerned by the sudden appearance and disappearance of two sweaty humans in rubber suits.

Mullion

The Plankton Trawl

We're in Cumberland Bay on the stern of the *Pharos* at dusk, about to start our first trawl. Only the net that is going off the back is no larger than a shopping bag and it isn't grown up fish that we are hoping to catch. British Antarctic Survey fishery biologist James is about to investigate the strange world at the bottom of the marine food chain.

Over the radio, James orders the trawl to start and casts his diminutive net. What comes back up is a greenish slush that on closer inspection is made up of a myriad of thousands of different tiny organisms. James wades through this marine soup with a pair of tweezers while on ship. He points out miniature crustaceans called copepods and the arrow and bristle worms that predate them. There are also krill and, crucially, the juvenile fish that help predict fishing catches a few years down the line.

After an initial inspection James preserves the catch in a glass jar of ethanol, dated in indelible ink, for proper analysis back at the lab. Once processed it will be added to the specimens storeroom together with goggle-eyed fish, underwater spiders and other outlandish sea creatures that populate these crammed shelves.

Plankton trawls are carried out in the same spot year on year to help assess the health of the fish stocks in South Georgian waters. The data helps the South Georgia government make informed decisions about what fish quotas to set. This is especially important for the slow growing Patagonian toothfish, caught with long lines up to 1,000 meters underwater. Fisheries science helps ensure that these waters, designated a Marine Protected Area in 2009, are some of the best protected from over-fishing in the world

Glacier Col

Museum staff member and experienced New Zealand mountain guide Sharon pauses at the apex of Glacier Col. We are standing on the last, smooth ice sheet at the inception of an all but vanished glacier, a brilliant bowl of reflected light, rimmed with loose stone.

All around there is evidence of the glacier's spent force. The rock is scarred and roughened by ice. Small lake basins and rounded knolls have been sculpted along the valley sides and lateral moraines mark the glacier's expansion and retreat through deep time. It feels like we are astronauts surveying some distant planet.

We head up towards a high spur of loose sandstone and mudstone for a view across to the Allardyce Mountains. It is a long climb on steep and unstable ground to reach the ridge but the panorama on the other side is astounding; splintered peaks, billowing cloud, fractured ice flow, a devilishly green lake. Somewhere in the island's interior an avalanche rumbles like a distant jet.

I slip into the deep silence in the lee of the summit and sense I've ventured too far into a world that holds no place for me. I feel weightless, as light as the Snow Petrel flashing its white wings on the thermals far below. For a moment I'm soaring with it from my craggy perch into the heart of this island's vast, Antarctic stillness.

St Andrews Bay

The visual spectacle is overwhelming, the noise deafening, the smell overpowering. Nothing could have prepared me for sitting on the beach at four in the morning in St Andrews Bay, surrounded by over 100,000 King Penguins. There are preening penguins, courting penguins, calling penguins, penguins feeding their young. Some are moulting, others waddling out of the pounding surf. A few are so full of squid and lantern fish that they lie like abandoned bowling balls on the beach, barely able to flipper themselves upright on the sand.

At the heart of the colony is the juvenile crèche, packed with awkward looking teenagers, covered in fine brown feathers. Kings only bring up two chicks every three years and the young take a year to fledge. This unique breeding cycle means that the colony is often courting, sitting on eggs and raising chicks at the same time. The result is constant commotion.

It is snowing and so cold that the battery is dying in my camera. And I don't have any idea where to point my camera because I can't take in anything beyond the sound and colour. Eventually I realise I have to step back from the clamour and stop looking at penguins. To see instead the entire colony and its surrounds as one interdependent entity.

I walk to higher ground and frame the beach, the river, the mountains and the colony in a single landscape. Taking an image like this is an act of faith. When a discordant world somehow pulls together and becomes whole again. I've never felt more present, as though my entire life has been leading up to this one, tremulous moment.

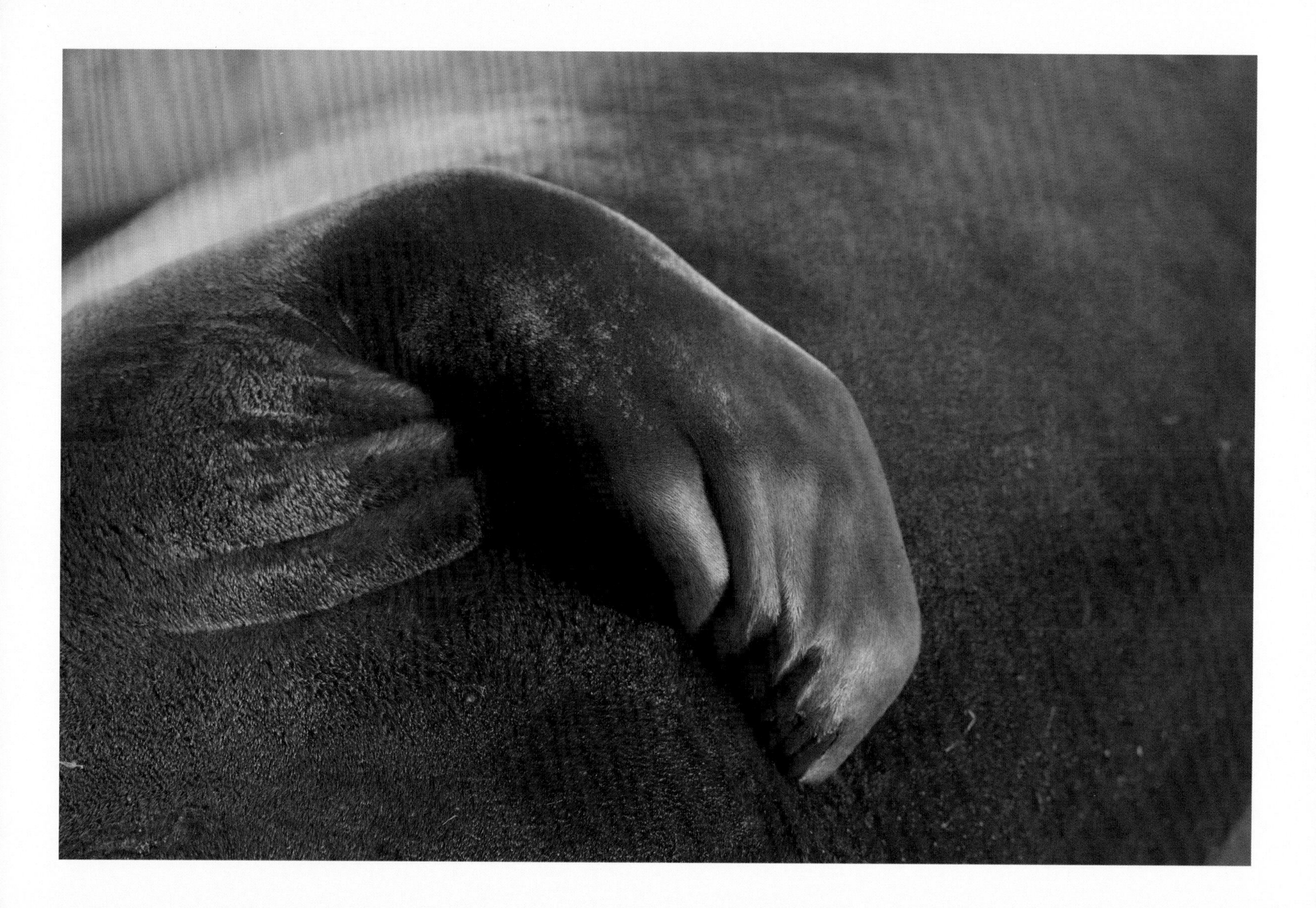

The Green

For all of South Georgia's mountainous drama it is easy to overlook the world carpeted at my feet. The climate may be too harsh for trees or shrubs but there is a jostling community of plant life underfoot. Many are endemic to the island and this forgotten frontier is home to hundreds of different mosses and lichens. So little has been mapped that botanists are still discovering new species of liverworts and algae every time they visit.

There is a treasure trove of abstract form to explore with a macro lens. So I spend a day seeking out small wonders on the aptly named Green Peninsula. I travel through yellow beds of stars, maps of lost continents, pixie cups and glinting beads on an emerald sea and return with wet elbows, my clothes covered in burrs.

Seeds are a big problem for the South Georgia Government. Some forty non-native plants have colonised the island from the whaling days when they were inadvertently brought on shore with cargo. Most are concentrated around the whaling stations but others like dandelion have been spread by the wind further afield.

With only 25 species of native 'higher' plants on South Georgia, the island's fragile habitats are vulnerable to invaders. There is an ongoing weed eradication programme and visitors now have to decontaminate clothes and bags in a bio-security area once they get onshore.

Whalebone Cove

There is a nondescript stony beach on the Green Peninsula that has become known as whalebone cove. Currents and tides have interacted to carry the bones that whalers threw into the sea at Grytviken across the waters to this remote corner. They are worn and bleached like driftwood and many have been colonised by lichens and mosses. It reminds me that we can't ever truly escape our own greed. Somehow the sea has brought these bones back, as if to say 'look what you did, look what you left behind.'

Winter Gifts

There is a long tradition on British Antarctic Survey bases of the over-winterers making gifts for each other. As time stretches with longer nights it is a chance to learn a new craft, or reconnect with an old one. The engineers' workshop at Grytviken, a cavernous space filled with offcuts and power tools, hums with music and gentle industry.

Here weird and wonderful things are honed. Glass coasters etched with personal messages, pens fashioned from ships timber, makeshift penguin key rings and deliberately pointless gifts like the useless box. Open it and a little hand pokes out to close it again. They may not be perfect but they are all unique.

I'm not lucky enough to experience a winter in South Georgia but I have made a little brass seal for my ten-year-old son. It was cast from a mould made by the Falkland Islands taxidermist and sculptor, Steve Massam.

Last Ascent

It is my last night on South Georgia and there is just time to ascend one last blue mountain. It is past midnight and we are in the bar at King Edward Point saying our farewells over a few drinks. I step outside and gaze up at Hodges in the moonlight. It looks like an imperious castle, cold and irresistible. So a few of us wrap up warm in the boot room and set off with just enough light to walk without head torches.

We scramble up a long ridge, feeling our way in places with our hands in the gloom, trying to beat the midsummer sunrise before we reach the top. As we quickly sober up our bravado ebbs and we settle for a windswept lookout on the saddle between Orca and Hodges. An orange tinge feathers across the horizon, catching the underside of high, lenticular clouds above Cumberland Bay. But we still have to wait out forty minutes of biting cold for the sun.

It is so hard to say goodbye to somewhere in the world as magical as South Georgia, but all the more bittersweet knowing that I most likely won't be back. Work and the challenge of getting here make this experience unique. I already miss the mountains and wildlife of this Antarctic isle, as well as the amazing friends who have also had the good fortune to venture out here to the ends of the world. The sun finally crests the skyline as I say one, final goodbye to South Georgia.

Summer in South Georgia picture captions

Title Page View across Hamberg Lakes from Glacier Col

p3 *Pharos SG*

p4 Cape Petrel

p7 Black-browed Albatross

p8 Dusk on the bridge of the *Pharos*

p10 Tabular glacier

p11 *Pharos* scanning for floating ice

p13 Bay of Isles

p14 Derelict whaling machinery at Grytviken

p15 Grytviken with Mount Hodges behind

p16 Moraine Fjord and Thatcher Peninsula

p19 Grytviken

p21 Whale-oil drums at Grytviken

p22 Foredeck of whale-catcher *Petrel* at Grytviken

p23 Whale catchers *Dias* and *Albatross* at Grytviken

p24 Baby Elephant Seals ('weaner' pups) play-fighting

p25 Male Elephant Seal with one of his females

p26 Wreck of the *Louise*, Grytviken

p28 Graveyard at Grytviken

p30 Mountain, Barff Peninsula

p33 Echo Pass, Thatcher Peninsula

p34 Harpon Hut

p36 Elephant Seals, St Andrews Bay

p37 Giant Petrel, St Andrews Bay

p38 Nesting Giant Petrel at Harpon

p41 Glacial ice, Harpon Bay

p42 Cumberland West Bay

p43 Lyell Glacier, Harpon Bay

p44 Discovery Point

p46 Sooty Albatrosses, Discovery Bay

p49 Zodiac, Cumberland West Bay

p50 Jet boat, Cumberland West Bay

p52 Harker Glacier, Moraine Fjord

p54 Suzanna's Hut at Carlita, Cumberland West Bay

p56 Carlita, Cumberland West Bay

p58 Cumberland West Bay

p60 Cumberland East Bay

p63 Nordenskjöld Glacier

p64 Sörling Valley, Barff Peninsula

p65 Cumberland East Bay and Nordenskjold Glacier

p66 Sailing around the Barff Peninsula

p68 Whale catcher *Albatross*, Grytviken

p70 Antarctic Fur Seal colony at Maiviken

p72 The Whalers' Church, Grytviken

p75 Unnamed peak above King Edward Cove

p76 Peaks between King Edward Cove and Maiviken

p78 Wetlands with seal

p80 Mount Osmond, Thatcher Peninsula

p83 The Horses' Plain

p84 Maiviken Lake

p86 Gentoo Penguin chick at Maiviken

p87 Gentoo colony on the Barff Peninsula

p88 Antarctic Fur Seal pup

p89 Maiviken Cove

p90 Corall Bay, Barff Peninsula

p92 Macaroni Penguin colony, Rookery Point, Barff Peninsula

p94 Macaroni Penguins, Rookery Point, Barff Peninsula

p97 Wandering Albatross

p98 Juvenile Wandering Albatross on Prion Island

p99 Boardwalk, Prion Island

p100 Landing the Zodiac at Prion Island

p103 Analysing plankton on the Pharos

p104 Mountain crossing, Barff Peninsula

p107 Mount Sugartop from Glacier Col, Thatcher Peninsula

p108 Author looking onto Allardyce Range and Glacier

p111 King Penguin colony at St Andrews Bay

p112 Juvenile King Penguins, St Andrews Bay

p114 King Penguin colony, St Andrews Bay

p116 Elephant Seals, St Andrews Bay

p118 King Penguins, St Andrews Bay

p119 Elephant Seal, St Andrews Bay

p121 Green Peninsula

p122 Lichen and moss, Green Peninsula

p124 Emerald green moss, Green Peninsula

p126 Whale bones, Green Peninsula

p129 Engineers workshop, Grytviken

p130 White Antarctic Seal

p131 Antarctic Tern

p133 First light on Orca, King Edward Cove

p135 King Edward Cove

Front Cover: Courting King Penguins, St Andrews Bay

Back Cover: Nine-pointed star on Sir Ernest Shackleton's headstone, Grytviken

Published in 2016 by
Watermill Books
Mill Street, Aberfeldy, PH15 2BG
www.aberfeldywatermill.com

British Library Cataloguing-in-Publication Data

A catalogue record for this book is available from the British Library

ISBN 978-0-9554358-9-8

Designed by David Harbott davidharbott@hotmail.com

Printed and bound under the supervision of
MRM Graphics, Wimslow, Buckinghamshire